Original title:
Oxygen and Verse

Copyright © 2025 Creative Arts Management OÜ
All rights reserved.

Author: Wyatt Kensington
ISBN HARDBACK: 978-1-80581-921-9
ISBN PAPERBACK: 978-1-80581-448-1
ISBN EBOOK: 978-1-80581-921-9

A Breath of Creativity

In a world where ideas float,
Like balloons, they can't be caught.
Witty thoughts fly around,
Tickling minds can't be bound.

A cartoonish tree with arms,
Swings ideas like it charms.
Silly squirrels wearing hats,
Share jokes with the acrobats.

Thoughts bubbling like a soda,
Make laughter dance in a moda.
Creative sparks light the air,
Filling the space everywhere.

Each giggle a puff, each grin a breath,
In this land, there's no such death.
Where humor reigns and grins will burst,
Awaken magic, quench your thirst.

Imagined Expanse

In a doodle of giant size,
Colors clash as fish wear ties.
A cake that glows with laughter's song,
Where muffins grow up oh so strong.

Rhythm tickles the floating pies,
As unicorns wear rollerblades, oh my!
Bubbles bounce on a trampoline,
In this realm, odd turns routine.

A snail wearing shades of bright hue,
Sprints by, and yes, it just flew!
In the garden, songs are spritzed,
Dancing flowers do the twist.

With every whiff of silly dreams,
The air thick with bakin' creams.
In whims, we soar with joy and cheer,
An imagined land, loud and clear.

The Pulse of Inhale

Inhale, exhale, dance with air,
Chasing bubbles without a care.
Lung balloons filled with giggles bright,
Who knew breathing could feel so light?

Noses twitch like a curious hare,
As we try to avoid sulfurous flares.
Choking on laughter, we leap and dive,
In the circus of breath, we're truly alive!

Harmony in Exhalation

A symphony played with every sigh,
But don't blame me if I start to cry!
Whispers of wind, a cheeky breeze,
This air in my lungs makes me wheeze!

The neighbors think I'm a kooky sprite,
Blowing bubbles from morning till night.
Who knew I could turn so absurd?
Inhaling giggles, I'm never deterred!

Ethereal Breath

With every puff, I feel so witty,
Floating like clouds, oh, isn't life pretty?
A grinning balloon, I rise so high,
Forget heavy thoughts, let laughter fly!

In the playground of air, I'm a kid once more,
Giggling fits make my belly sore.
Stretching my lungs like elastic bands,
Exploring the world with my silly plans!

Cadence of Clouds

Airy verses tumble and roll,
Who knew inhaling could tickle the soul?
Puffing out poems in a comical flurry,
With laughter as fuel, I need not hurry.

My breath's a melody, a whimsical tune,
Singing with stars under the moon.
Riding the waves of exhales and sighs,
Every chuckle a gift, a surprise to the skies!

Whispers of the Wind

Laughing leaves in trees, so spry,
They tickle noses as they fly.
Breezes giggle, play a tune,
While clouds dance to a funny rune.

Squirrels chatter, what a sight,
Breezy banter, pure delight.
Branches sway in comic flair,
Nature's jesters everywhere!

Lyrical Lungs

Inhale a giggle, exhale a cheer,
Chasing bubbles, isn't it dear?
A hiccup here, a snort or two,
Our lungs always planning something new.

A sneeze like fireworks, loud and bright,
Lively sighs to start the night.
Sing through your nose, let laughter soar,
Breath's a party, come get some more!

Songs in the Atmosphere

Whistles slide and giggles glide,
In the air, a playful ride.
Banana peels and kite tails chase,
Harmony meets a clumsy embrace.

Traffic lights wink as birds chime in,
A duet formed from a silly grin.
Echoes of laughter fill up the sky,
Mistakes become hits, oh my, oh my!

Chasing Aether

Bubbles pop and dreams are spun,
Chasing gleeful clouds, oh what fun!
Kites laugh too, they soar so high,
While butterflies wink as they pass by.

Every breath a tiny giggle,
As laughter dances, set to wiggle.
A symphony of whimsy, we're afloat,
In the laughter-filled air, let joy emote!

Aetherial Reverberations

In a world where thoughts take flight,
Words bounce around, a joyous sight.
Bubbles of laughter burst in the air,
Silly rhymes dance without a care.

Giggles and grins, a playful spree,
Invisible whispers tickle a tree.
Airy antics frolic in the breeze,
Each line a tickle, sure to please.

Plumes of Poetry

Witty puffs of creativity soar,
Like clouds of cotton, they giggle and roar.
Jokes in the mist, they flutter and sway,
Each line a puff, brightening the day.

Silly thoughts sprout like flowers in spring,
Chasing the mundane with a playful fling.
Stardust of laughter, we let it rise,
Words playing hide and seek in the skies.

Floating Beyond the Ordinary

Whimsical notions drift on a breeze,
Painting the air with colorful keys.
Mirthful echoes bounce off the walls,
As laughter in currents merrily sprawls.

In this realm where the wild things roam,
We conjure up smiles, no need for a home.
Doodles of dreams hang on a string,
Silly secrets that make our hearts sing.

Rise of the Daydreamer

Up in the clouds where thoughts take flight,
A daydream awakens, shining bright.
Juggling ideas like a circus clown,
Witty inventions wear a silly crown.

Bouncing through realms of nonsense and glee,
Dancing with shadows, wild and free.
The sun winks cheerfully, inviting the fun,
A chorus of whimsy for everyone.

Chords of the Celestial

In a sky full of blue, the birds take a dive,
With a squawk and a flap, they joyfully arrive.
They dance through the clouds, with flair and with grace,
While I watch from below, with a smile on my face.

Stars make a racket, with twinkles and shouts,
They throw amazing parties, with no room for doubts.
The moon plays the drums, the sun sings a tune,
It's a cosmic cabaret, while I'm stuck with a spoon.

Expression in Euphoria

Ticklish laughter fills the air, it's all around,
While cosmic balloons bounce off the ground.
With each giggle and snort, life becomes a ride,
At a carnival fair, we let our joy glide.

Jellybeans dancing, oh what a sight!
With marshmallow clouds that float up in delight.
We'll paint the sky with flavors so sweet,
In our swirling world of humor and heat.

Flight of the Spirit

Butterflies flit, on a mission to tease,
In a whimsical chase, they move with such ease.
While I try to catch them, and flail like a fool,
They laugh at my antics, but hey, who's the cool?

Each tumble and twist sends me spinning around,
Like a spinning top, I'm lost and then found.
The world does a jig, and so do my socks,
With giggles and wiggles, we ignite laughter's clocks.

Luminescence of Living

Neon lights flashing, a party on foam,
With fish on skateboards, they've called it their home.
They twirl and they glide, on rollerblade fins,
While I munch on some popcorn and laugh at their spins.

A comet zips by, in a cloud of confetti,
Chasing a nightingale, all sweet and heady.
The world is a playground, so wild and so bright,
With each tickling moment we spark pure delight.

Fluidity in Breaths

Inhale the giggles, hold them tight,
Exhale the chuckles, take to flight.
With every puff, a joke takes shape,
Filling the air, like an invisible cape.

Laughter bubbles in the playful breeze,
We share our quirks, doing as we please.
A symphony of snickers fills the space,
While silly faces dance with grace.

Bubbles of mirth float high and low,
Twirling and swirling, taking a bow.
Guffaws erupt like unexpected storms,
Drawing us close in their joyful forms.

So breathe in deep, let laughter flow,
With each puff, let hilarity grow.
In this merry dance, we must delight,
Finding humor in the day and night.

Poetic Exhalation

A puff of nonsense, a wheeze of fun,
Breathe in the laughter, let it run.
Silly rhymes sneak into the light,
Turning blunders into pure delight.

With every breath, a tale unfolds,
Of socks mismatched or dreams so bold.
Giggling whispers echo around,
In our silly world, joy is found.

As we exhale each playful line,
The air vibrates, it feels divine.
Poetic stutters tickle the air,
We breathe in jest, floating on flair.

So huff and puff, let the whimsy rise,
In a world where humor never dies.
Every giggle is a breath we share,
In this merry realm, we're light as air.

The Essence of Expression

What's that smell? Is it steam or smoke?
No, it's laughter — the best kind of joke.
With each word, we puff and cheer,
Creating a storm of happy veneer.

A whispered jest, a comedy flare,
We inhale smiles, floating on air.
Curly mustaches and goofy grins,
In our fun-filled world, everyone wins.

With every chuckle, a bubble pops,
Who knew humor could reach such tops?
Tongue-twisters dancing, all in their prime,
Breathless, we giggle, losing all time.

So let's fill the air with playful yells,
With quirky tales and funny smells.
In a world where laughter takes its claim,
We find pure joy, never the same.

Chasing the Wind

We race the breeze with jokes in tow,
Chasing the wind like a circus show.
Inhaled jests spark a silly chase,
Our lungs filled with glee, smiles on our face.

Each gust carries wit, quick as a sprout,
Silly puns bubble up, no doubt.
With every breath, mirth swirls around,
As we prance and laugh, joy abounds.

Floating phrases, a whimsical ride,
The funny breeze becomes our guide.
A dash of humor, a sprinkle of zing,
In this lovely dance, our hearts take wing.

So let's breathe in the playful tide,
Chasing the wind, side by side.
Together we thrive in this laughter spree,
As we flutter like leaves, wild and free.

Unseen Currents of Thought

Whispers dance in the air,
Tickling nostrils with flair.
Ideas float, sly as a cat,
Making minds wonder, 'What's that?'

Inhale the giggles of bees,
Exhale the tickles and wheezes.
Thoughts bounce like popcorn in pots,
Who knew pondering was such a plot?

Breezes tease with their jest,
Leaving logic in quite a quest.
Seriousness takes a backseat,
As we giggle, quick on our feet.

So here's to the air that we share,
Where humor floats without a care.
Each thought a bubble, bright and bold,
In this dance, our laughter unfolds.

Breathless Reflections

In the mirror, I see my grin,
Puffing air, where to begin?
My thoughts race like a train on track,
Stopping only to giggle and snack.

Reflections bounce off the wall,
With each chuckle, I feel tall.
My brain's a circus, wild and free,
With clowns juggling all 'round me.

Thoughts are balloons filled with glee,
Floating high, just wait and see.
Each one pops with a silly sound,
As I laugh, my worries drown.

What's serious must have been lost,
As I ponder, at what cost?
With breathless fun in every thought,
Here's the joy that life has brought.

Dancing with the Drafts

Wisps of air twist and twirl,
Like a dancer in a whirl.
Each gust brings a brand new laugh,
As we join in the playful calv.

Drafts of giggles fill the room,
Time to wiggle, shake off gloom.
Swaying lightly with the breeze,
Finding joy like floating leaves.

In every puff, a joke's concealed,
Like playful secrets long revealed.
My thoughts spin, a merry chase,
As I dance with a silly grace.

So come sway with me, my friend,
On this laughter we depend.
With every breath, a chuckle shared,
In this playful moment, we are paired.

Fluid Verses

Words float like bubbles in a stream,
Each one pops, igniting a dream.
A silly thought or a quirky pun,
A joyous race, we've just begun.

Flowing freely, like a breeze at play,
Tickling ideas, whisking away.
Laughter spills over in bright cascades,
As we water the humor that never fades.

Verses wiggle, twist, and clap,
In a whimsical, playful map.
With each line, a splash of fun,
Making poetry second to none.

So let's craft a world that's light,
Where every chuckle feels just right.
In this dance where humor converses,
We find delight in fluid verses.

The Essence of Being

Inhale the laughter, exhale the fun,
Life's a bubble, a joyous run.
Our thoughts dance wildly, like squirrels on a spree,
Breathing in giggles, oh how carefree!

Tickling your insides, a whimsy delight,
Bouncing like jelly in the moonlight.
With each silly moment that bounces around,
We're floating on bubbles, blissfully unbound.

How do we manage this buoyant affair?
With snorts and chuckles, let down your hair.
Like balloons in the sky, we rise with a grin,
Exhaling all worries, let the fun begin!

So take a deep breath, let your spirit soar,
Join the parade, the laughter galore.
With each playful puff, joy fills the air,
We're giddy, we're silly, it's magic we share!

Notes from the Nurtured

In a garden of chuckles, we plant our dreams,
With every hiccup, the sunlight beams.
The daisies giggle, the daisies sway,
As we sing our hearts out, come what may.

Watering laughter, with humor we grow,
Planting the seeds of delightful woe.
The caterpillars wiggle and dance in the sun,
They're sashaying through life, just having their fun.

Butterfly wishes take flight in the breeze,
While we drop our troubles like autumn leaves.
With each titter and tinkle, our spirits ignite,
In this bubbling garden, everything's bright.

We weave our stories with whimsical threads,
Where laughter is planted, no room for dreads.
So, let's have a picnic, with snacks made of cheer,
Nurtured by giggles, we've got nothing to fear!

Clouded Chronicles

In the skies of whimsy, our fancies roam,
Floating on giggles, we're far from home.
We craft our tales on marshmallow fluff,
Spinning our stories, never too tough.

Puffy clouds whisper, little secrets untold,
As rainbows erupt, bright and bold.
With laughter as ink, we scribe in the air,
Each bounce of the heart brings stories to share.

Pirates of giggles sail storms of delight,
Chasing sunbeams, from morning till night.
With a wink and a nod, our tales take flight,
Fluffy adventures in clouds so bright.

The horizon chuckles, with each passing day,
As we play in the clouds, in our own silly way.
With hearts made of laughter, let the winds spin,
In these clouded chronicles, we find the win!

Puffs of Potential

Whimsical wisps float through the air,
Tickling our noses, without a care.
With each little giggle, we pave the way,
For puffs of potential to frolic and play.

Dancing on breezes, like dandelion fluffs,
Each puff a promise, it's never enough.
The world is a canvas where silliness spreads,
Creating a tapestry from chuckles and reds.

Let's skip down the path of our dreams today,
With laughter as fuel, we'll find our way.
Each puff an adventure, a playful delight,
As we bounce through the hours, our spirits take flight.

So gather the giggles, and blow them around,
With puffs of potential, let joy abound.
In the festival of laughter, together we'll cheer,
For each little giggle makes the world dear!

Life's Lingering Notes

In the garden of thoughts, I sneeze,
Chasing breezes with such ease.
Words dance lightly on the air,
Riddles float, with nary a care.

Giggles twirl like dandelion seeds,
Spreading laughter, planting good deeds.
Each chuckle's a bubble, ready to burst,
In the symphony of life, we all thirst.

Silly voices, they wiggle and wave,
Squeaky sounds, the soul to save.
Nonsensical rhymes in a zany spree,
Tickling ribs, we're wild and free.

So let's inhale this whimsical play,
Exhale the worries, let them sway.
Life's lingering notes, let's hum along,
In this frolicsome concert, we belong.

Elysium of Breath

In a realm where giggles soar,
A pufferfish starts a laughter war.
Bubbles rise, with ticklish flair,
Each pop sends joy rippling through the air.

Snickering clouds, they huff and puff,
Witty jests, never too gruff.
With every grin, we share delight,
Turning mundane into sheer flight.

Quips and quakes, the sky's our stage,
We perform with flair, we're all the rage.
Like a joke that tells itself anew,
In this elysium, we're never blue.

So take a breath, let humor ignite,
Let's tumble into the starlit night.
Together we'll weave this tapestry of fun,
Fun's our fuel, we'll never outrun!

Breath of Words

A whisper of wit dances around,
Jokes take off without a sound.
Laughter pirouettes, light as air,
Floating freely, without a care.

Each pun like a kite, soaring high,
Tugging at giggles, flying by.
With every chuckle, the world's aglow,
Sprinkling joy like confetti in flow.

Sighs of laughter, a symphonic spree,
Mirthful melodies, just you and me.
In this frothy breeze, we find our place,
Breath of words, a jubilant embrace.

So let's exhale the heavy and dark,
Inhale chuckles, let's make our mark.
In this fanciful dance of ours,
We breathe in harmony, like blooming flowers.

The Air Between Us

In this quirky realm we share,
The air's thick with comedic flair.
Every glance a playful tease,
Like a sneeze that won't cease.

With witty banter, we float along,
In the breeze, we find our song.
Tickles rocket through the space,
We take off, in joy's embrace.

Mirth hangs low, a fragrant plume,
Essence of joy begins to bloom.
The mirthful moments, they entwine,
Building bridges through laugh's design.

So let's release our burdens tight,
Gather giggles, hold on tight.
In this lightness, we'll find the truth,
The air between us, a fountain of youth.

The Vital Flow

Inhale the giggles, they fill the air,
Exhale the worries, let go of despair.
Bubbles of laughter, a fizzy delight,
Dancing like fireflies, twinkling at night.

Wheezing with joy, we tumble and roll,
Chasing the breeze, it tickles the soul.
Sneeze of surprise, oh what a show,
Who knew that silliness could steal the glow?

Puffing like dragons, we blow out our grins,
Giggling so hard, we startles the pins.
Floating on puffs of comic delight,
We juggle our chuckles, oh what a sight!

In the playground of laughter, we swing and soar,
With every good pun, we always want more.
Breathing in folly, it's a wild ride,
Our hearts full of giggles, we cuddle inside.

Floating on Fragments

Bubbles in the air, like thoughts on a spree,
Each one a riddle, what could it be?
Frolicking fragments of dreams in our minds,
Like playful kittens, they leap and unwind.

Sipping on whimsy, oh what a taste,
Floating through time, never in haste.
Tickling the fancies, oh what a tease,
A carousel of chaos, spinning with ease.

With giggles like glitter, we brighten the lanes,
Chasing down starlight, ignoring the rains.
Side-splitting madness, we draw from the skies,
Each burst of laughter, a joyous surprise.

We dance on the edges of silly and wise,
With noses in the air, we gaze at the skies.
Fragments of humor, stitched with delight,
Together we bubble, our spirits ignite.

Woven in the Wind

Threads of hilarity tangled in glee,
A tapestry woven, just you and me.
Ticklish whispers, they flutter and twirl,
Like dandelion wishes, they dance and swirl.

Kite-stringed laughter, soaring so high,
Catching the clouds, giggling shy.
Each stitch a snicker, each knot a grin,
In this fabric of fun, we both dive in.

Breezy exchanges, come join the leap,
Jumping through moonbeams, into the deep.
Quilting the moments with yarns of cheer,
We craft our delight, year after year.

Woven in the wind, we flutter and float,
On laughter's soft currents, we drift and gloat.
With every bright whim, we stitch and we seam,
In the quilt of our laughter, we live our dream.

Harmony in Hues

Brushstrokes of laughter in colors so bright,
Splashes of whimsy, a painter's delight.
Jubilant rainbows blend red, blue, and green,
Each hue a giggle, like nothing we've seen.

Chortles like cerulean, tickles of gold,
A canvas of fun, bright stories unfold.
Painting with joy on life's grand display,
With heartwarming laughter, we laugh all day.

Sunshine in pastels, we skip and we sway,
Each chuckle like brush strokes, come join the play.
A splash of absurdity, a wink and a smile,
In this gallery of glee, we'll linger a while.

Harmony pulses in every stroke made,
As giggles blend gently in colorful parade.
We'll paint the world joyful, with each merry view,
In the realm of delight, forever anew.

Syllables of Renewal

Inhale the goofy sounds, so bright,
Words dance like sprightly sprites,
Every syllable a burst of cheer,
Laughter's air, we hold so dear.

Puns float like bubbles in the sky,
Tickling senses as they fly,
A breeze of wit, a gust of glee,
Verbal acrobats, wild and free.

Voices giggle, chatter, and play,
In the wind, they twist and sway,
A comedy show in every breeze,
Laughter blooms like flowers of tease.

The air is thick with mirthful sound,
In every corner, joy is found,
As silly rhymes chase clouds away,
We tip our hats to the absurd play.

Echoes in the Ether

Whispers wiggle in the air,
Jokes ride high without a care,
Every chuckle sends a shiver,
Banter flows like a happy river.

Silly puns bounce off the walls,
Hilarity rings, and so it calls,
Come join the frolic in this land,
Where laughter's currency is unplanned.

We shout to clouds, they giggle back,
In this realm, there's never lack,
Echoing whimsy in the breeze,
Foolishness is sure to please.

As voices rise and dip and swirl,
A calypso of mirth begins to whirl,
In this atmosphere, light and free,
We craft our joy with sheer glee.

Lyrical Breaths

Take a breath; it's rhyme o'clock,
Words are peeking out from the block,
They juggle concepts like a clown,
Painting smiles all over town.

Letters leap like kangaroos,
Making mischief, spreading hues,
In every line, a funny wink,
In the air, we laugh and think.

Each twist of phrase—a playful tease,
Jests float up like autumn leaves,
In the breeze of whimsical prose,
We find the fun; we strike a pose.

Let's skip along this jovial path,
Crafting laughter, feeling its math,
For every giggle in the night,
Is a breath of joy, pure delight.

Messages in the Mist

Fog rolls in with a cheeky grin,
Muffled giggles start to spin,
Whispers float, entwined like lace,
A mystery wrapped in a playful space.

Riddles tumble in the thick haze,
Bantering softly, like playful rays,
Clouds chime in on the fun parade,
As secrets dance in the masquerade.

Words swirl 'round like drifting leaves,
Tickling our minds, like well-earned reprieves,
In this shroud of joy, we delight,
Crafting laughter, day and night.

So take a step into the blur,
Find the giggles and let them stir,
In the mist, the laughter sings,
Messages of mirth on playful wings.

Musing in the Ether

Floating thoughts like feathers,
Tickle the nose with laughter.
The sky is just a goofy place,
Where brains do cartwheels after.

Clouds wear socks, a sight to see,
Dancing on the whimsy breeze.
Whispers of dreams in silly tones,
Giggles escaping with perfect ease.

Roots of Reflection

Gnarled roots of a tree so wise,
Tell jokes with their leafy sighs.
Conversations with bugs so small,
They bumble along and never stall.

Each branch a tale of grand delight,
As shadows wiggle in the light.
A world where even raindrops cheer,
Making puddles full of sneers.

Sighs of the Universe

Stars wink at us from afar,
Twirling like a fancy car.
Galaxies giggle, they can't help it,
Shooting stars in a cosmic skit.

Each planet in a tutu spins,
While moons perform and pull the sins.
A chuckle echoes through the night,
As comets flash, a dash of light.

Inhaling Inspiration

Breathing in a zany breeze,
Tickling minds like a swarm of bees.
A whiff of whimsy, a dash of cheer,
Ideas bloom while giggles appear.

Laughter bubbles in the air,
Crafting dreams with a funny flair.
Each breath a canvas, so divine,
Painting smiles with every line.

Cadence in Clarity

In a world full of chatter, it's hard to see,
The whispers of air are free as can be.
Floating through giggles, we dance on the breeze,
Sipping on moments, we're giggling with ease.

Breathe in some laughter, let out a cheer,
It tickles the insides, it's so crystal clear.
With each silly hiccup, the rhythm takes flight,
Jumping on clouds, we're giddy tonight.

The rhythm of life is a syncopated spree,
A chorus of chuckles as we spin with glee.
No need for a script, just follow the sound,
In this cacophony, joy can be found.

Float like a balloon, don't touch the ground,
With each puff of humor, new friends can be found.
So join in the frolic, don't hold your breath,
In this bubbly ballet, we wink at death.

Inhale the Silence

In a quiet room where giggles reside,
A sneeze starts a party, you just cannot hide.
The air fills with whispers, and then with a roar,
As silence erupts, it's laughter galore.

Every exhale is painted with glee,
Like bubbles that pop, it's quite the spree.
We tread on the tiptoes of barely-held sighs,
And burst into chuckles, no need for goodbyes.

Let's snicker at stillness, we're cheeky and bright,
Inhaling each moment, we heighten delight.
With winks and soft chuckles that bounce on the air,
We're composing a symphony, silly and rare.

This hush that surrounds us, a delicate nest,
Invites silly antics, and loosens our zest.
So take in the quiet, exhale with a grin,
In this silent ruckus, let the fun begin.

Vowels in Flight

A, E, I, O, U, take to the skies,
Winging their way through the chortles and sighs.
Frolicking vowels, on letters they ride,
With laughter as fuel, they swirl and glide.

Sipping on giggles, they fill up their tanks,
Ooo-ing and aah-ing, they soar with their pranks.
They loop through the air, in an acrobatic spin,
Dancing on syllables, let the games begin!

Their antics are witty, they tickle the ear,
Making the mundane feel joyous and clear.
Each flap of their wings makes a raucous cheer,
With every bold whisper, the nonsense draws near.

So come join the chorus, let vowels ignite,
A cacophony of fun, take off in delight.
With humor suspended, let's laugh and unite,
As we follow our dreams, on the winds of the night.

Rhythm of the Breeze

Breezes at play, with a rhythm so sly,
They dance through the trees, where the squirrels comply.
Chirping and chuckling, they tickle the leaves,
As patches of laughter float in and then leave.

A tickle of breeze, a nudge in the air,
With every small gust, we all stop and stare.
Giggling branches sway, a harmonious croon,
As humor crops up like a jolly balloon.

The sway of the grass keeps time with our hearts,
Each rustle a punchline, where silliness starts.
So chuckle along, let the fun set you free,
In the rhythm of whispers, we'll float joyfully.

When breezes are playful, we join in the tease,
With laughter as sunlight, we warm with the breeze.
Let's skip through the layers, where laughter can squeeze,
In the dance of the moment, we find our sweet ease.

Verse Born from Vapors

In the morning, I took a breath,
My cat coughed, it's like a theft.
I gasped and laughed at the surprise,
While bubbles floated 'neath the skies.

We danced around in fragrant air,
While socks disappeared, a true affair.
My neighbor sneezed, startled the cat,
And soon we had a bubble spat!

The goldfish swam with elegant flair,
Chasing dreams in a dreamy chair.
With every puff, a joke unfurled,
In our swimming pool, we twirled!

A vapor here, a giggle there,
In clouds we found a playful lair.
Words floated by like feathers bright,
In our whimsical world of light.

The Pulse of Poetry

A beat, a skip, a merry sound,
Where rhymes and giggles all abound.
The cat starts tapping on the fridge,
While I think thoughts, as big as a bridge.

I tried to write on a windy day,
My page flew off, oh what a play!
It landed far, on a dog's head,
Who looked quite puzzled, as I read.

My coffee dripped on my big foot,
And with each jolt, my mind took root.
With every sip, a stanza brewed,
In clumsy rhythms, I was hoodooed.

The streetlamp winked, the sky did sigh,
As verses danced and tried to fly.
I penned my lines with fleeting haste,
In this silly world, no time to waste!

Nuances of the Skies

Clouds wore hats made of fluff and cream,
While shadows whispered a playful dream.
The sun threw coins of yellow light,
And I caught one, what a sight!

Birds dressed sharp in dapper suits,
Singing tunes with funky roots.
My shoes did squeak like a funny tune,
As I twirled beneath the afternoon.

A butterfly slipped on a banana peel,
While I chuckled at the surreal.
With each tickle from the breeze,
My laughter soared with greatest ease.

Each hue a giggle, each shade a grin,
The world spun fast, let the fun begin!
In every nuance, joy takes flight,
Under the sky's whimsical light.

A Gentle Current

A breeze tickles as I stroll,
Chasing leaves, that's my goal.
The creek gurgles a silly sound,
While splashing fish leap all around.

I wore my flip-flops, one fell away,
And danced on toes, oh what a play!
The ducks quacked loudly, threw their sass,
I giggled back, they joined my class.

A squirrel jumped, surprised my face,
With acorn snacks in a frantic race.
With every step, my laughter grew,
In nature's rhythm, each line was new.

The sun dripped down like honey won,
As evening came, my joy was spun.
In the current, we twirled with glee,
Nature's dance, so wild and free!

Attunement to Existence

In the garden where leaves dance,
I try to cha-cha with a plant.
It roots for me, I take a chance,
But all that twirls is just a pant.

Breath in bubbles, float them high,
A jellyfish asks why I sigh.
I tell him tales of sky and pie,
He giggles and says, 'Give it a try!'

I exhale stories, thick and sweet,
About the neighbor's pet parakeet.
It dreams of heights on tiny feet,
While surfboards make the air complete.

Underneath this cosmic caper,
I wrestle with the world's great paper.
The ink spills out, a funny draper,
Spaghetti stars in satire's taper.

Shreds of Sky

A cloud of cotton candy swirls,
While birds compete with gossip twirls.
One says the sun's unfurling curls,
The others argue, flapping pearls.

On rooftops, laughter floats like air,
My neighbor's cat sings out a dare.
To jump the fence and flirt with flair,
But what if I forget the stair?

As shadows stretch and giggles blend,
A squirrel shares its acorn trend.
'Try wearing hats,' it grins, my friend,
'Then watch your woes take off and bend!'

Amid the shreds of azure light,
I find my muse in feathered flight.
They quack and flap, a joyous sight,
We're all just figments, free and bright!

Epiphany in the Ether

Floating thoughts like balloons in the breeze,
I question the ants, if they feel at ease.
They march with purpose, without any keys,
While I trip on words, like clumsy peas.

A whisper from the clouds says, 'Be a bee!'
I buzz around, sipping honey from tea.
I laugh at my reflection in the tree,
It winks back at me, a cheeky spree!

Puns drop like rain, and giggles arise,
Each chuckle is wrapped in a disguise.
The leaves join the party, swaying like flies,
While squirrels debate the merits of pies.

In this space full of playful glee,
The universe spins, as silly as me.
Every thought a whirl, every joke a decree,
I'll take a bow, then sip on my tea!

Brilliance beyond Boundaries

Wobbling on the edge of the world,
With cosmic spaghetti all unfurled.
I slip on stars, and laughter hurled,
What a treat! This madness swirled!

I chase a comet, but what a plight,
It turns around, giving me a fright.
'Why the rush? Just sample the light,'
It winks like a joker, sudden delight!

Galaxies giggle, exchanging puns,
While planets play hopscotch, having fun.
A meteor shower; catch just one,
It's a wishing game, we all can run!

In this space where reason is lost,
The humor's rich, and joy's the cost.
Let's dance with the quirks, no matter the frost,
In brilliance beyond, we're never crossed!

Symphony of the Unsung

In the air, there's a tune,
Invisible notes that make us swoon.
Fish in the sky, they're quite the sight,
Swapping their fins for wings of light.

Clouds are just puffs, a comedy show,
Juggling the sun, putting on a glow.
Every breath is a raucous cheer,
A celebration of life that's oh-so-clear.

Chasing the whispers, we dance and sway,
In our own playhouse, come what may.
Feathers of laughter, tickles of glee,
Floating and fluttering, wild and free.

So take a deep breath, let joy explode,
In this bubbly world, take the happy road.
With giggles in every inhaled delight,
We'll serenade the stars every night!

Stanzas in the Stratosphere

Floating high, like a balloon,
Words go up to meet the moon.
Giggling clouds in a rowdy cheer,
Who knew the sky could be so sheer?

Chirpy birds in a rhythmic dance,
Sipping on breezes, taking a chance.
Each line a hop, a jig, a twist,
In this high-flying joyful mist.

Tickling tongues with airy rhymes,
Swapping breath like borrowed times.
Feel the hiccup of farty winds,
Life's too playful to have any sins.

So let's compose, oh what a scene,
In the upper world where the laughter's keen.
With every sigh, let the fun unfold,
In this ballooning tale, we'll be bold!

Lingers in the Transparency

A bubble of giggles, escaping a laugh,
Floating around, it's a whimsical path.
Hiccups of joy in a clear disguise,
Kite-flying dreams gaze through the skies.

Transparency's folly, a joker's delight,
Wobbling wonders take glorious flight.
Tickle your senses, let them all sway,
In this nonsense where we laugh and play.

Clouds wearing coats of cotton fluff,
Dancing through wrinkles, isn't that tough?
Delighted wisps tease the sunlight's hair,
Each giggle is fragrant, light as air.

So let's leap forth on this transparent spree,
Crafting our stories for all to see.
In this playful realm, oh how we spin,
Like marshmallow dreams on a lollipop whim!

Exuberance in Emptiness

In a vacuum, the jester's call,
Bounding about in a weightless thrall.
Bubbles of laughter snicker and tease,
In this void where we dance with ease.

Floating nothings, it's quite divine,
Every exhaled joke tastes like wine.
Guffaws and snorts in the endless blue,
Who knew that empty could feel so true?

Echoes of silliness bounce and play,
Absurdities crafted in a grand ballet.
From giggling orbs to whimsical spins,
Life's sparkling moments where joy begins.

So shout in the void, let your spirit fly,
With buoyant hearts, we reach for the sky.
In the realms of nothing, we find our cheer,
Where every chuckle brings the world near!

Threads of the Invisible

In the air, there lurks a thread,
Tickling toes and fluffing your head.
Invisible gas, making us giggle,
While we try to solve the world's widdle wiggle.

Balloons float by with a cheeky grin,
Mocking the science we're all stuck in.
They twist and turn, dodge and weave,
As if to say, "You'll never believe!"

A sneeze erupts, a laugh breaks free,
"Excuse me, how rude!" says the poor bumblebee.
But as we puff and sway with delight,
We dance like dandelions, in sunlight so bright.

So take a breath, join the fuss,
In this crazy world, don't make a fuss.
With invisible threads, we laugh and weave,
Creating a tapestry, hard to believe.

Spirals of Sentiment

A swirl of joy, tangling about,
In ribbons of laughter, there's never doubt.
Spirits rise as we twirl and spin,
In this breath of life, we all begin.

A ticklish breeze plays hide and seek,
As we chase the giggles, fate feels so bleak.
Funny shapes in clouds above,
Whisper secrets of silly love.

With every puff, a chuckle shared,
In the playful air, we're unprepared.
So let the humor bubble and rise,
And fill our hearts with joyful sighs.

We spiral up on laughter's wings,
In this breathy song, the heartstrings sing.
So grab a smile and don't hold back,
We're on a wild and funny track.

Dawn of Discovery

The sun peeks in, and what's that smell?
Fresh coffee brews; it casts a spell.
A yawn escapes, I stretch, then grin,
Ready for adventures to begin!

Who knew a breeze could bring such cheer?
Making pigeons dance as they squeal near.
The world wakes up, giggling awake,
What other wonders will we partake?

A curious squirrel with a hat too tight,
Doing the cha-cha, such a sight!
While flowers bloom in colors so bright,
Chasing bees 'round, oh what a flight!

In this dawn of discovery, we find our way,
With laughter and fun, come what may.
Let the day unfold like a giggly song,
In this world of surprises, we all belong.

Ascending into Thought

Up we go on thoughts that soar,
Bouncing around, can't help but explore.
Like bubbles in a fizzy drink,
We giggle and float, it makes us think.

With every gasp, a new idea flies,
Tickling our minds, oh my, what a rise!
They dance like fireflies, up in the night,
In this mental space, everything feels right.

A comic twist, a ponderous plight,
As we climb higher into pure delight.
With laughter as our guiding thread,
We turn the mundane into sheer bread spread!

So let your thoughts leap, jump, and twirl,
In this whimsical dance, let the fun unfurl.
With each inhalation, wisdom we catch,
Ascending into thoughts, there's no match!

Harmonizing with the Haze

In the air floats a giggle,
As bubbles bounce with glee,
I tried to swim in a puddle,
But ended up in a tree.

Clouds are fluffier than jelly,
I'll dance on a fluffy mound,
Gigantic birds with tiny hats,
Keep spinning round and round.

Breezes whisper silly tunes,
In a language made of hums,
I tap my feet in rhythm,
While wondering where it comes.

With every breath, I chuckle,
At the silly stuff I find,
Like chasing down a sunbeam,
And leaving all strife behind.

Meditations in Motion

I sat upon a cloud one day,
To ponder life's great style,
But then it sneezed, oh what a spray,
A drizzle of sunshine and a smile.

Trees started swaying in the breeze,
As if they all took ballet,
They pranced and spun with such pure ease,
While I just giggled away.

Leaves laughed as they swirled around,
In colors bright and bold,
Nature's own circus to astound,
With stories to be told.

In every breath, the funny flows,
In this lively, free ballet,
Breathless, I join nature's shows,
And forget my cares for the day.

Wandering Wisps

A wisp came drifting by my nose,
And tickled me with glee,
I sneezed aloud, the humor flows,
And set that wisp to flee.

As shadows danced on streams of light,
The trees began to laugh,
And fireflies took to the night,
With stars in their own craft.

I chased after a glowing laugh,
But tripped upon a rock,
Fell into a marshy path,
Where frogs all laughed in shock.

Yet still I rise, with merry grin,
To find where giggles roam,
For every flow has a fun spin,
And laughter leads me home.

Cascading Cadence

A stream began to hum a tune,
As pebbles joined in play,
I marveled at this nature's boon,
While I tried to sway.

The trees clapped hands, the birds did sing,
In symphonies of cheer,
The sky wore shades of purple bling,
And sparkled bright, I fear.

Then a butterfly flipped the beat,
With flutters strange and sweet,
I stomped my feet, forgot my seat,
As nature moved my feet.

In every breath, the rhythm swells,
Each giggle fuels the space,
In this grand show where joy compels,
I dance without a trace.

Breath of Stanzas

Inhale the words, what a delight,
The syllables dance, taking flight.
Puff out the rhymes, let them soar,
A giggle of verses, asking for more.

Playful breaths in every line,
Tickling tongues, oh how divine!
Sneeze out a pun, let it glide,
With laughter sprouting, side by side.

Chuckle with commas, giggle with glee,
Every phrase a joyous decree.
Swirl in hilarity, twist and sway,
In this merry poem, let's all play!

A wheeze of whimsy, a snicker or two,
Words banter back, as if they knew.
A chorus of chuckles, echoes so bright,
In this playful breath, we unite!

Lungs of Language

A puff of phrases, oh what a breeze,
Tickling ideas, aiming to please.
Inhale the nonsense, exhale the fun,
Each word a monkey, on the run!

Bubbling up giggles, flowing like air,
Chasing the dragons that dance without care.
A rush of nonsense, what a delight,
Filling up pages, taking flight.

Gasping for meaning, in laughter we drown,
A symphony of sounds, in this quirky town.
Building tall castles of whimsical prose,
With each silly line, the laughter only grows.

Wheezing through stanzas, the joy never ends,
Each verse like confetti, as the laughter extends.
We breathe and we joke, let the fun unfurl,
In the lungs of language, watch our jests twirl!

Whispering Atmosphere

Whispers of whimsy, soft as a sigh,
Floating like feathers, way up high.
A giggle drifts, on currents it rides,
In this airy realm, where humor abides.

Ticklish whispers, cheeky and bold,
Stories unfold, but only if told.
A breeze of banter, swirling with cheer,
Each ripple a chuckle, loud and clear!

Hitching a ride on the breeze of a joke,
Crafting a melody, playful yet woke.
Laughter entwined in the lightest of air,
In this whisperscape, we frolic and dare.

Floating on laughter, what a sweet sound,
In the soft atmosphere, joy can be found.
With every soft chuckle, every smile shared,
This whispering realm has us all ensnared!

The Air Between Words

In the gaps of chatter, where giggles reside,
The air holds secrets, a playful guide.
Whispers of joy float, bubbling up high,
Crafting a riddle that tickles the sky.

Gusts of laughter tease, say what they will,
A tickle of humor, a light-hearted thrill.
Dancing on syllables, bouncing around,
In this breezy banter, joy can be found.

Puffs of nonsense, swirling all day,
Catch them like bubbles, watch them play.
Between every line, a chuckle awaits,
In the air of our words, joy radiates!

So take a deep breath, let giggles ignite,
In this playful space, everything feels right.
With a wink and a smile, let the fun unfurl,
In the air wrapped in words, we dance and twirl!

Sonnet of the Sky

Up in the clouds, a bird lost its map,
Searching for snacks, it fell in a flap.
Pigeons all giggled, they pointed and stared,
As he tried to fly but said, 'My wings are impaired!'

Rainbows erupted—what a silly sight!
A cat on a cloud wrestled with light.
The sun wore sunglasses, shining the way,
While the moon chuckled softly, 'I'm out for the day!'

In the grand playground of air and delight,
Bubbles of laughter filled hearts with pure light.
Each breath a joke that floats here and there,
So let's joke with the breeze, dance without a care.

At dusk, the horizon painted in cheer,
While stars throw confetti, oh what a sphere!
With each joyful gust, we flap and we glide,
In this circus of wonders, we'll take it in stride.

Vital Rhythms

The trees are nodding, they know how to groove,
With branches that sway, in a cheeky move.
Leaves rustling playfully, sharing some laughs,
While bugs throw a party and show off their halves.

In the deep of the night, the crickets compose,
Symphonies buzzing, nobody knows.
With each little chirp, they tickle our ears,
A concert of giggles that lasts through the years.

The flowers all chuckle with colors so bright,
Tickling the air with sweet scents of delight.
In gardens of wonder, we burst into dance,
With each vital breath, we embrace every chance.

So let's join the rhythm, tap feet on the ground,
In the pulse of nature, our joy can be found.
With laughter like bubbles, we float through this game,
In the vital heartbeats, we're all just the same!

Melodies of the Mist

Morning mist giggles, wrapping things tight,
Dancing with shadows, oh what a sight!
Whispers in fog, a tickle of breeze,
As I trip on a dew drop, oh please, oh please!

Curly-haired clouds want to play and they sway,
With laughter that floats, in their fluffy ballet.
A crow drops a joke, it lands with a thud,
And everyone snickers, 'Oh what a dud!'

The sun peeks through, a grin on its face,
As flowers all blush in their soft, cozy space.
Melodies ripple through branches and vines,
In the laughter of mist, pure joy intertwines.

And when evening falls, all is light as a feather,
As the stars play a game, we all laugh together.
In the sweet serenade of nature's sweet jest,
Each moment a giggle, life's funny quest!

Echoes of Embrace

In the forest's arms, where echoes unite,
Laughter bounces back, it's a marvelous sight.
The squirrels share secrets, all giggles and cheer,
While the owls look puzzled, 'What's that over here?'

Trees swap tall tales, twisty and grand,
Of acorns and leaves, oh, can you understand?
The breeze acts like a jester, spinning about,
With a whoosh of delight, never a doubt.

Down by the brook, the water will chat,
With pebbles that giggle, and fish that say, 'What?
You fished for a tale? Well, let's take a dive!'
And they splash your shoes, saying, 'Aren't we alive?'

In this circle of laughter, we nurture and share,
Each moment a hug, wrapped up in fresh air.
As echoes of joy resound through the trees,
With every warm breeze, we can't help but tease!

Tranquil Footprints

In the park, I stomp and play,
Chasing butterflies that flit away.
Each footprint leaves a quirky trace,
Laughter echoes in this silly space.

The squirrels laugh, they know the game,
As I tumble down, what a shame!
They mock my dance, a funny sight,
Nature's stage, pure delight.

In puddles, I splash with glee,
Creating waves, just you and me.
The ducks quack, they join the fun,
Together, we bask in the sun.

My shoes are soaked, what a day,
But who needs dry when you can play?
I leave behind my happy prints,
In this wild dance, the world hints.

Weaving Whispers Across Time

In the quiet, whispers roam,
Tickling ears like a wandering gnome.
Time giggles as it skips along,
Dancing softly to a silly song.

Sticky notes with jokes appear,
Caught in the moments we hold dear.
Each chuckle chains the minutes fast,
Moments weave like a spell we cast.

A laugh escapes and time takes flight,
In this comedy of day and night.
History chuckles, oh so sly,
As we stumble and give it a try.

The clock winks with a knowing grin,
Reminding us where we've been.
For every giggle, every cheer,
Threads of joy pull us near.

Pages in the Air

A breeze carries stories to the sky,
As paper planes flutter and fly.
Each fold a giggle, a twist of fate,
Wings of laughter, can't be late!

In the winds, our dreams take flight,
Chasing clouds with sheer delight.
Books in hand, we laugh and cheer,
Pages swirling, drawing us near.

With every breeze, a tale is spun,
Adventures wait, so let's have fun!
We toss our worries to the air,
Trusting the wind to take our care.

Each catch is clumsy, a funny dance,
As letters float, they take their chance.
In the chaos, joy ascends,
Crafting laughter that never ends.

Fragments of Serenity

In the midst of chaos, peace appears,
Laughter bubbles, calming our fears.
Tiny moments, like fireflies,
Whispering jokes beneath the skies.

In a world that spins and swirls,
Serenity twirls with funny curls.
Each pause a chuckle, soft and sweet,
Finding calm in our silly feet.

The teapot whistles, steam takes flight,
While spoons dance in pure delight.
Tea spills over, what a scene,
Fragments of peace, so comically keen.

Through every giggle, the storm subsides,
In laughter's arms, joy resides.
So here's to moments, light and free,
Crafting fragments of harmony.

www.ingramcontent.com/pod-product-compliance
Lightning Source LLC
Chambersburg PA
CBHW071127130526
44590CB00056B/2814